THE CELTIC CHAKRAS

A concise and elegant introduction to a Celtic way of understanding reality. Elen Sentier appreciates the depth of meaning present in the myths and riddles of the British Isles and makes an erudite and entertaining guide for the curious seeker.
Lyn Webster Wilde, author of *Becoming the Enchanter* & several other books; OU tutor

Rich with personal vision, the book is an interesting exploration of wholeness. Drawing on stories and traditions that are central to modern Pagan and New Age thinking, Sentier finds a deep and valuable root within the spiritual heritage of Britain.
Emma Restall Orr, author of *Living With Honour* and *The Wakeful World* etc.

Elen Sentier takes us on a well-considered journey, weaving Celtic lore and sacred geometry with experiential practices that move us into heart-full embodiment of ancient wisdom. The *Celtic Chakras* is a multi-dimensional and dynamic exploration of the body's energy system, illuminating a sacred pathway to evolved human consciousness.
Llyn Roberts, a prominent teacher of healing and shamanism, is the award-winning author of *Shapeshifting into Higher Consciousness*. Llyn also wrote *The Good Remembering* and *Shamanic Reiki*.

Dance to the centre with Elen Sentier's groundbreaking *Celtic Chakras*, an enlightening synthesis of ancient shamanic lore, wisdom, journeys and meditations for the beginner or seasoned practitioner alike...enter the world of the ancestors, of Elen of the

Ways, Arianrhod, Ceridwen, and more... From the Heart to the Brow, the unique spiral path of Celtic wisdom can lead one through the chakras in a special way, a guide to illuminating the Still Point within. Highly recommended.

Dr Karen Ralls, author of *Templars and the Grail, Sacred Doorways,* and *Music & the Celtic Otherworld*

Shaman Pathways

The Celtic Chakras

Shaman Pathways

The Celtic Chakras

Elen Sentier

Winchester, UK
Washington, USA

First published by Moon Books, 2013
Moon Books is an imprint of John Hunt Publishing Ltd., Laurel House, Station Approach,
Alresford, Hants, SO24 9JH, UK
office1@jhpbooks.net
www.johnhuntpublishing.com
www.moon-books.net

For distributor details and how to order please visit the 'Ordering' section on our website.

Text copyright: Elen Sentier 2011

ISBN: 978 1 78099 506 9

A CIP catalogue record for this book is available from the British Library.

Design and cover photograph: Stuart Davies
www.stuartdaviesart.com

Printed and bound by CPI Group (UK) Ltd, Croydon, CR0 4YY

We operate a distinctive and ethical publishing philosophy in all
areas of our business, from our global network of authors to
production and worldwide distribution.

CONTENTS

Also by Elen Sentier

Moon Song

Owl Woman

Toad in the Shadow Lands (novella & short stories)

Dreamweaver (shamanic how-to book)

Numerology: the Spiral Path

What are the Celtic Chakras?

Some people think there is no concept of "chakras" in the western tradition but this is not the case. Chakras are not a purely eastern concept but one found throughout the mystery traditions all over the world. I was interested to read what writer and novelist, Jim Donaldson, says on his website, "*As ancient mythologies, apparently so idle and meaningless, are now perceived to embody truths, scientific and religious, so the seemingly foolish traditions of nations, descriptive of their early history, are recognized to convey ideas more or less astronomical and theological.*" It's good to see other folk coming to realise that what has been scorned by academics in the past is very far from the rubbish and children's fantasies we were told it was.

There is a strong body of *knowing* of the energy centres, and the pathways between them, that the cunning folk and spirit keepers of Britain have known from time out of mind but, in the way of all esoteric and occult traditions, it is very well hidden in the stories and song of this land. This book takes you to follow the quicksilver pathways of the goddesses Elen of the Ways, Arianrhod, Ceridwen and Fraid and so discover the ancient wisdom for yourself.

The eastern systems have for many years been quite well known; our western systems have been hidden in story, song and old lore. From years of reading, studying and experimenting with willing people I've been able to go deeply into the ancient stories of our land and figure out from their riddling what they tell about how the Earth works. That's what Grammarye is about; it's the old word for the lore, the wisdom teachings, used by cunning folk and I'll be using the word in this book. Grammarye is a system to help us find and remember how the world works, how the whole fits together. It's what physicists and mathematicians are working towards too. When you can get to talk to them privately, as I've sometimes been able to do, they freely admit that there is a lot of correspondence between what they see and think and the old stories of our planet. I've worked with many of the traditions from around the Earth, eastern and western; when you sit with them, ponder them, hold several threads together in your mind, you begin to see how they say the same thing, how their grammarye is of the whole world but expressed differently depending on the spirit of place who is guardian to that part of the Earth. Grammarye helps us to get into the sense and feeling of the land, brings us closer to the ancestors who hold the wisdom for us and expand our own knowing.

I find I'm asked two questions when I first talk about the Celtic chakra system …

- How are the Celtic Chakras different from the eastern systems? I thought the word was Sanskrit and they were only an eastern concept.
- All the books I've read go through the chakras from the base up to the crown. Why do the Celts use a spiral?

Spiral Path

Stories are the main way for the Celtic shaman to learn grammarye, the lore, we follow the spiral path of story, never going straight at a thing but always following the twists and turns of the path. Elen of the Ways, the ancient reindeer goddess of the northern peoples who haunted the Boreal Forest (of which Britain was a part) and her sister goddesses show us the tracks and pathways for our lives.

The triskele spins and spirals its way through the Celtic chakra system. It threads its way through Celtic art but it is much more than just a beautiful pattern, it holds one of the fundamental principles of the Celtic spiritual and mystery tradition, the 3-in-1.

There are three main forms of path for humans to walk through the spirit worlds; the straight line, the circle and the spiral.

- The straight line is simple linear time; from birth to death; folk tend to think of it as a progression each step following on the previous, continuous expansion from a point of nothing-ness (like the Big Bang theory).
- The circle is also time; cycles and seasons, returning always to the same place.
- The spiral contains both the cycles and the sense of progression but without the restricting points of either continuous outward expansion or continual return to the same place. It has a sense of breathing; a sense of continuity *and* newness ... the *and/and* principle rather than the exclusive *either/or* that many folk live with.

The mathematician Kurt Gödel's *theorem of incompleteness* expresses this nicely for our modern age and those who like a scientific correspondence (like me). Our ancestors knew but expressed it differently and perhaps more poetically. They knew and saw and worked with the spiral that happens throughout the natural world, from sunflower seeds to chakras.

The spiral path leads you through the chakras in a special way. The principle of spiral movement is fundamental in the Celtic tradition; you find it throughout art and stories. Perhaps the most famous Celtic symbol, the triskele, the threeness patterns you find in Celtic art, shows it best. The old saying, "a picture's worth a thousand words", was well known to our ancestors; here are some examples of Triskeles.

All of these are ways of showing us, giving us the grammarye, the structure of the web, the wyrd. The chakras within our

Troy Town

bodies and within the land are a fundamental part of this.

The major difference with the Celtic system is that it works in a *spiral* rather than a linear fashion and is always dual – breathing in/out, feminine/masculine, all the pairs of opposites. The ancient labyrinth known as the Troy Town does this too; it spirals in then spirals out, continually; this is the way the energy goes both *through* and between the chakras and *within* each chakra.

This can be a bit hard to get one's head around so the best thing to do is to give one's head sixpence and tell it to go out to play, so giving the intuition space to work. Throughout my life I've always found that *experiential* learning is the most effective, both for myself and for the people I work with ... do it first then talk (and think) about it once you have the experience inside you. On that note, let's try a short journey to walk the spiral path through the chakras.

Journey: the Spiral Path

Unlike the way most teachers tell you to go, the Celtic shaman does not journey simply from bottom to top, following the rainbow colours. The Celtic shaman always works in spirals: this way you get to meet the chakras in the pairs (cauldrons) in which they function.

You *spiral* round and out from the centre, *not* from bottom to top. So ...

Begin at the **heart** centre; sense, feel yourself centred in the heart; spend a few moments there getting to know the feel of your heart centre, see it new as though you had never seen it before. When you are ready, see a silvery thread going out from your heart. Follow the quicksilver path DOWN to the Heart's partner the **solar plexus**.

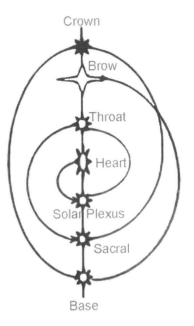

Chakra Spiral

Spend a few moments with the **solar plexus**, sense, feel yourself centred in there; get to know the feel of your solar plexus centre, see it new as though you had never seen it before. When you are ready, see a silvery thread going out from your solar plexus. Follow the quicksilver path UP to the **throat centre**.

Spend a few moments with the **throat centre**, sense, feel yourself centred in there; get to know the feel of your throat centre, see it new as though you had never seen it before. When you are ready, see a silvery thread going out from your solar plexus. Follow the quicksilver path DOWN to the **sacral centre just below the belly button**.

Spend a few moments with the **sacral centre**, sense, feel yourself centred in there; get to know the feel of your sacral centre, see it new as though you had never seen it before. When you are ready, see a silvery thread going out from your sacral centre. Follow the quicksilver path UP to the **crown centre**.

Spend a few moments with the **crown centre**, sense, feel yourself there. You may find it quite entrancing so do your best to stay grounded; it is an amazing place and connects you directly to otherworld. It's very important NOT to drift off, *not* to "go with the flow", you need to stay with it and be able to continue your journey for you are by no means done yet. When you are ready, see a silvery thread going out from your crown. Follow the quicksilver path DOWN to the **base centre** at the base of your spine.

Spend a few moments with the **base centre**, sense, feel yourself centred in there; get to know the feel of your base centre, see it new as though you had never seen it before. It too can seem entrancing although usually less devastatingly than the crown. The base centre connects to the heart of the Earth so is also very powerful. Don't get stuck there, be ready to move on for you are still not finished with your journey. When you are ready, see a silvery thread going out from your base centre. Follow the quicksilver path UP to the **brow centre**.

The **brow centre** is another amazing place. It is where all the threads from the other six centres come together and are integrated into a wholeness that is you in this lifetime. One of the phrases many folk use to describe it is the place of "bright darkness". At first, this seems to be a paradox, how can darkness be bright? When you actually go there by doing this exercise you'll see what it means, finding the words to describe it is far harder than actually knowing it. Spend a little time there but, again, do NOT get lost!

When you are ready to leave, thank the brow and all the centres for showing you themselves and say you will visit them again to learn more.

Now it is time to come home, to return to the everyday world. Take a deep breath and sigh it out, take another and sigh that out too, and a third. Swallow, move your mouth, wiggle your fingers and toes, rub your hands together then rub your knees and legs and arms, have a good stretch and a yawn, then open your eyes. Blink a few times, move your head gently on your neck, hunch your shoulders and let go, rub your feet on the floor. When you feel that you're safely back in your body thank your body for being there for you to return to.

Make a few notes and drawings to remind you of your journey then make yourself a warm drink and have something nice to snack on. You may not realise it but you've done a lot of work just in that simple-seeming journey and you need to replenish your body for the energy it gave you while you worked.

This come-back routine is very effective, we'll use it for all the journeys.

The Abred: Three Realms

The ABRED is a Celtic symbol already in use five thousand years ago. Three circles of the same size overlap to form a centre, representing the totality of being. It is a Power-shape, a shaman's tool. It represents the three spirit worlds and realms, at their three levels. It contains ...

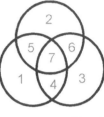

Abred

- In the outer ring you have the single parts – 1,2 & 3 – of the 3 circles
- At the next level you have the double parts – 4,5 & 6
- In the centre, 7, you have the place where the 3 circles all overlap and become one

This is what the Triskele is expressing.

All of this wisdom and grammarye is built from the simple drawing of the 3 overlapping circles. Our Celtic forebears were particularly good at fitting a quart into a pint pot!

In Celtic lore the Three Realms are named *Ceugent* (ky-gent, hard g), *Gwyned*, and *Abred*.

The following table of correspondences is useful to see how things relate.

CEUGENT 1st Realm	GWYNED 2nd Realm	ABRED 3rd Realm
Upperworld,	*Middleworld,*	*Underworld,*
Red light	Blue light	Green light
Smith	Healer	Poet
Maiden	Mother	Crone
Life	Consciousness	Mind
Cauldron of Warming	Cauldron of Vocation	Cauldron of Wisdom
Crown/Base	Heart/Solar Plexus	Throat/Sacral
Power	Love	Wisdom
Red Cup of Lordship	White Cup of Fostering	Black Cup of Forgetfulness

Journey: Torch Exercise – 3-ness

This is a fundamental exercise for you; doing it is a consciousness-changing exercise.

You need –

- 3 light-sources (lamps, torches) that each create a spot of light on the wall.
- A white wall or other uncoloured surface to project onto.
- 1 red, 1 blue and 1 green gel to cover each of the lights. Preferably use theatre lighting gels as their colour is very strong, but any art shop should be able to help.
- Set the light sources up to all point at one spot on the wall – this is important, spend time on it, if the lights don't overlap you won't get the full effect.
- Put a coloured gel onto each light-source.
- Turn on the lights, one at a time …
- WATCH the colours change as you add each light
- When all three are pointing at the same spot, what colour is the light on the wall?
- It should be White … if it isn't jiggle the lights around until they are all aligned, all covering the same spot on the wall, from the same distance, then it will be white. Take time and

have patience with yourself over this, it's important for you to see it.

- Alignment has big implications ... spend time getting it right.
- When you have the white light, pass your hand between the torches and the wall ...
- What happens on the wall?
- What happens on your hand?

Do this several times until you are fairly clear in your mind what is happening.

You should be seeing rainbow-shadows on the wall as you pass your hand between the lights and the wall. You should also see rainbows on your hand.

This exercise shows you the three lights symbolising the source, the three-ness, of the triskele. The wall is like the Earth. In order to form colour and shape, to show differences, know boundaries. The white light is first split into its component parts by Movement, Beingness, Living, that dances between the source and Earth. This movement splits the light into the myriad rainbow colours of Life.

This is shown by the movement of your hand. The colours change both on the wall AND on your hand; so you are changed by the movement as the earth herself is changed by the movement.

Life is movement, change, continually dancing. The *Dineh* people, the Navajo, call it *dammas*, meaning "that which moves". It's known all over the world and called by different names; the awenyddion, the cunning folk, the shamans, dance, shift in the light, making patterns, shadows, helping reality to BE.

Elen of the Ways

Who is Elen of the Ways?

This is an enormous question; in another book I give you a far deeper experience with her but, for the moment, we'll stay with her work with the Celtic chakras.

Sir John Rhys calls her the *goddess of Twilight* because her times are the dawn and dusk. *She is goddess of "between the two lights",* gateways to the ways between worlds. She is often portrayed as an antlered woman. Amongst deer only reindeer females carry antlers and reindeer once ran on British soil. They also pull the gift-bringer's sledge at the Midwinter festival.

Elen is best known through the Mabinogion tale, The Dream of Macsen Wledig. Macsen was also known as Magnus Maximus, called the British emperor of Rome, and is an actual historical figure. He wedded a British princess, Elen, who was one of the Faer, an otherworldly woman, not human but goddess and sovereign in her own right and thus able to grant sovereignty to her partner, thus making him one of the symbolic guardians of the land.

The story of their union is told in the Mabinogion, the old Welsh collections of grammarye. Briefly it goes as follows ...

Macsen was a Roman general of Spanish descent who dreamed of the most beautiful woman in the world, wished to find and marry her. It took a long time, the magical seven year quest, but finally he found her in her father's caer (stronghold) up on the northwest coast of Wales, by the otherworldly island of Mona and in the sacred land of the Eagle (Snowdon). He woos and weds her. As her wedding gift Elen asks him to build her three caers (castles, strongholds) with three roads linking them all together. The roads are called *sarns* in Welsh and there are traces of them still in the landscape at some of the sacred sites. After seven years, as the story tells it, Macsen goes to conquer Rome and becomes emperor, with the aid of Elen's brothers. Eventually, supposedly in 388AD, Theodosius I defeats Macsen's army in battle; he is captured and executed at Aquileia.

However, the point of the old story is not to tell history but to teach grammarye.

Elen as Sovereignty

Elen is an otherworldly woman, a goddess; she is called Sovereignty in the British tradition. This signifies that she is the spirit of the Earth, of the Land in its totality; she holds the threads, the web that is the Earth. Macsen is her guardian, the husbandman who keeps the Earth for her.

All through the Celtic tradition goddesses and gods come in pairs; they hold the feminine and the masculine, the pairs of opposites out of which creation is made. This is duality ... without which nothing is manifest and all remains potential. To use a correspondence with the Tao, Elen holds the Receptive principle while Macsen hold the Creative principle; to translate that across to the Celtic way, the receptive is the Cauldron or Grail, the Creative is the Spear or Sword. In British royal regalia the receptive is the orb and the creative is the sceptre which are fundamental to the coronation of our sovereigns (note the use of the word again). The principle goes back to honouring the womb and penis of human creation and can be found all around the world.

The Celtic tradition holds this concept very deeply; this is why, to us, all things have spirits that hold each of the two energies ... including the chakras. The Troy Town spiral holds this principle too; you go into the centre of the labyrinth, then you come out again by the same path but in the other direction; just like the male principle entering the vagina and the sperm entering the womb, then the created spirit emerges from that centre.

The following table of correspondences will give you some ideas …

Queen = Spirit-self	King = personal self for each incarnation
The Land	Guardian
Wife	Husbandman
The Field	Tiller of the Field

Duality: Queens & Kings

What are queens and kings in the British Celtic tradition?

Elen was *always* a queen, she didn't have to wed with Macsen to become one. In fact *he* had to wed with *her* to become a king, before that historically he was military governor of the Roman province of Britannia This is how it is in the Celtic spirit tradition; the queen confers royalty onto her spouse, thus making him a king. The goddess, the Earth, gives life and regality to all of her creation, it comes out of the womb of Life. The king, the masculine principle, is guardian. You can, if you wish, follow through all the etymology of the many words for wife and queen through language, it's a fascinating journey but not one I'm going into here. The point that we need to be clear about for the chakras is that …

- they *contain* the duality that is Life
- the queen, feminine, is paramount and the masculine is the guardian of this principle.

The queen in the Celtic physical world is the representative of the goddess, priest if you like; she carries the energy for us. The king is her guardian, *not* her lord. One British tradition that shows this – although well hidden in the modern day, as are many spirit-truths – is the Morris Dance tradition. The Morris side, the dancers, are the queen's men, "Mary's men" with the name

"Mary" signifying water, the sea, the life-principle ... we cannot live without water! John Matthews' work on this concept is enlightening if you want to follow the idea further.

Troy Town

One of the old *testings* in Britain was running the labyrinth, the Troy Town. It's a labyrinth of seven turns that takes you both widdershins and deosil from the outside to the centre ... and then from the centre back to the outside.

The Troy Town labyrinth is the spiral that also holds the duality of the Lady and the Lord, the goddess and the god. The goddess' priestess would run to the centre then the candidates for her guardian would run the labyrinth to find her. This is told in songs like the Fith Fath song or the Coal Black Smith; they are not rape-songs but tell of the goddess setting tests for the god; if he can catch her then she will keep him.

This spiral occurs in the Celtic chakras. As I said, many people find their way through the chakras from bottom to top, or top to bottom, but that's not the Celtic way; the Celts start at the centre and spiral their way outwards. As you found in the journey, the Celtic way begins at the heart and threads its spiral way down through the solar plexus, up to the throat, down to the sacral, up to the crown, down to the base and finally up to the brow.

The brow is the meeting place that holds all the energies of the chakras. It's often drawn as a lemniscate. This is about the duality again, two petals, one holds the energy of the Lady and the other holds the energy of the Lord. The

Lemniscate

spiral winds in and out, turning, turning, widdershins, deosil, carrying the duality, the coming together of the two that makes the One.

Duality & Spin in the Chakras

DUALITY; centripetal/centrifugal, masculine/feminine, is a basic part of the structure of the chakra. Each chakra holds the two poles, the queen and king, the duality that enables life to manifest. They are two sides of one coin. In our everyday world the spirit-self carries the queen-energy, our personality-self carries the king-energy.

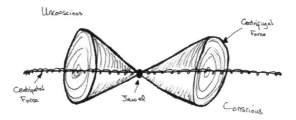

Chakra

This diagram is a good *functional* map of a chakra and shows the duality (it's not what a chakra actually *looks* like but it *is* how it works). The two spinning cones meet at their points; each cone spins in the opposite direction from the other – duality again.

Through the centre of the cones passes what appears as a rod. Like the double helix of DNA it, too, spins in both directions at once and each end of the rod spins in the opposite direction to the cone it passes through. It is a multiple expression of duality. It reminds me of the figure "the hay" in country dances where the men and women go round the circle in opposite directions and weave in and out of each other as they go round, touching hands as they pass. The old dances hold the old grammarye-knowing too.

The rod carries the inward spin of *centripetal*, masculine, energy; it pulls the spin inwards in a tight, one-pointed, penetrating way, like a spear. The cone carries the centrifugal, feminine, energy which throws outwards in an expansive, inclusive way like a great whirlpool, cauldron or cup.

The meeting of the energies at the central point to be causes that point to be *both* still *and* chaotic at the same time. It is the place of change ... and of wholeness.

Bob Toben's book "Space-Time and Beyond" has a couple of excellent diagrams that expand on this idea of the chakra.

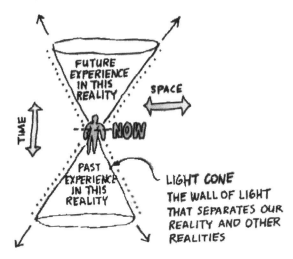

Herman Weyl - Double Cone

The 20th century German mathematician, Herman Weyl (1885-1955) says *"Every world point is the origin of the double-cone of the active future and the passive past ... so that, in principle, it is possible to experience events now that will in part be an effect of my future resolves and actions."*

So you have past-and-future, unconscious-and-conscious, inner-and-outer world, all connected through the rods and the cones. The central point is the place of interchange; the black hole, the centre of the chakra; as the old rede says, "As above, so below".

It is a gateway of consciousness that the cunning folk, the awenyddion, the British spirit-keepers, along with all shamans, use to walk between worlds. It seems very similar to how scientists describe the black-hole/white-hole phenomenon; you pass through what, from this side, appears to be a black hole then, when you view it from the other side, it appears as a white hole. As you pass through this door/gate your perspective is reversed.

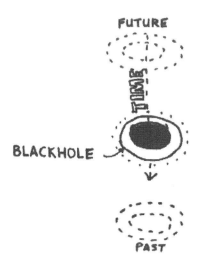

Black Hole

Duality in the chakras

Coiling your way along the quicksilver paths through the pairs of chakras is the reason you travel through them in a spiral, starting from the centre and working outwards and inwards, outwards and inwards, outward and inward to arrive at the place (the brow) where the three pairs combine into the seven-fold energy, into oneness.

Your journey takes you from ...

- Heart to Solar Plexus to
- Throat to Sacral to
- Crown to Base to
- Brow ... where all are integrated, again into the duality of the pairs of opposites.

QUEEN	KING
Heart	Solar Plexus
Throat	Sacral
Crown	Base

Brow: where the Queen and King are wed

Pairs of Chakras

One of the principles Elen holds for us is Duality, we've explored her relationship with Macsen Wledig – where she holds the spirit-self principle while he holds the guardianship of that spirit-self, the jobs of the queen and the king. We've talked about how this principle of duality is carried in the chakra, how it spirals in with the masculine, penetrating energy, and spirals out with the feminine, expansive energy; and how this is shown in the Troy town labyrinth.

The Celtic tradition is about the wedding of the pairs of opposites. This picture comes from a Celtic gold ornament discovered in a woman's tomb at Bad Durkheim in the Hunsruck-Eifel area, Germany dating to the late 5th century or early 4th century B.C. It expresses the lady/lord very well. If you look at the picture one way up you see the face of an old man; if you turn the picture the other way up you see the face of a young woman. Always there is the lady and the lord. This is the basic duality through which our Earth works; goddess and god, holding the pairs of opposites. Our ancestors didn't separate off the life of spirit as we do nowadays; everything was part of Life, part of the whole, not one bit for Sundays and another style for the rest of the week.

It's worth looking at the pairs of opposites again, they come in everywhere. The pairs of opposites are each side of one coin ... as our ancestors showed in the engraving on the ornament, the old man who becomes the young woman who becomes the old man, again and again as you turn the brooch.

Dark/Light
Feminine/Masculine
Receptive/Creative
Womb/Phallus
Orb/Sceptre
Stigma/Stamen
Cup/Athame
Grail/Spear
Inner/Outer

These are just a few examples, I'm sure you can find more for yourself. Each chakra holds this duality, and each pair of chakras holds it too.

3-ness: Caers, Castles & Cauldrons

So, back to Elen ...

As her bridal gift, Elen asks Macsen to build her three Caers; he does this and the caers are said to be at what are now Caer y n'Arfon (Caernarvon), Caer Leon (Caerleon) and Caerfyrddin (Carmarthen). They symbolise the three pairs of chakras each of which holds this creative/receptive energy which enlivens us all. This energy is the same triple energy that Brighid holds – Blacksmith, Healer and Poet which we'll talk about in her chapter later on.

Elen's three Caers symbolise the three pairs of chakras and

carry the energy of the Three Cauldrons of Poesy ...

Caer y n'Arfon	*Crown/Base*	Life
Caer Leon	*Heart/Solar Plexus*	Vocation
Caerfyrddin	*Throat/Sacral*	Wisdom

Caer y n'Arfon is the castle that looks across the worlds, to Mona, one of the Isles of Glas (like Glastonbury) and a place of the Faer. It spans between heaven and earth, enabling us to walk between the worlds, as do the crown and base chakra pair; they give *life*

Caer Leon is the place of the flowing waters. It is built at the lowest crossing point of the sacred river Usk. The flowing of the waters and their regular flooding is about how our love can enable us to do the job we promised our spirit-totem-group we would do in our current incarnation. This is our *vocation*, our life-path.

Caerfyrddin is the stronghold by the sea, the castle that holds and stores the *wisdom* of the ages. Myrddin (spelled fyrddin here) is another spelling of Merlin. One of the old names for the island of Britain was Clas Myrddin, the place of Merlin; Britain is the stronghold surrounded by the sea, another form of this Caer. Merlin is the wise one who knows and guides the kings.

This three-ness is told again in the Gaelic poem, The Cauldrons of Poesy, which we will explore with Ceridwen.

Caers are strong places where a people could hold together in times of stress (not always or necessarily war but also bad winters, drought, famine or disease). Back in ancient times our ancestors made enclosures; some contained in earth banks, some marked by stones, sometimes daub-and-wattle walls were built on the banks. Our modern, separatist natures lead us to jump to conclusions that these must have been defensive structures, built for war, but a little deeper thought shows that this is unlikely. Hunter-gatherer folk do not "own" land; they are guardians to the land but not owners; they work *with* the Earth rather than trying to control and manipulate her to make money and profit, and for their own small ideas of the common good. Hunter-gatherers know and respect the land and all her creatures and plants; they hunt for food, following the herds; they collect plants and fruits and nuts by season rather than trying to extend seasons and force the land to produce what they want. Until farming there was no need for war to take or hold land; and, until farming, the human population remained stable, in balance with the Earth and her seasons; until farming there was no need for more than replacement children who would be loved and respected rather than bred as a workforce. Even pastoralists worked this way, *with* the land rather than raping her; for a fairly recent example of how folks in touch with the land lived look at how the native tribes of Yellowstone lived before Cornelius Hedges, of the Washburn expedition, proposed that the region should be set aside and protected as a National Park.

Caers are about places where folk gathered. From many years' work (since the early 70s) with ley and energy lines I've found they occur at places where many earth-energy threads come together, a nexus of threads, making a strong place. They are like chakra points in the Earth. The chakras in our bodies, and in the bodies of all living things, are places where energy threads come together – a super Clapham Junctions of the energy tracks that make us.

So, Elen's caers are symbols of the three main junction points where pairs of chakras meet, where the queen and king energy (feminine and masculine) meet. They are strongholds of this energy, refuges and retreats where this double-helix energy is held.

Elen's Ways

When Macsen – the guardian spirit – had built the Caers, Elen made pathways between them. These roads are the pathways between each Caer, each holds one of the pairs of chakras; the paths are similar in function to the nadis and meridians of the eastern traditions. They carry the energy between each of the chakras in each pair and between one pair of chakras and another. In the body of the Earth herself they are the dragon, song and ley energy lines connecting the many chakra points of the sacred places.

The paths spiral. The spiral is fundamental to the Celtic tradition as it is in many others (e.g. the Navajo); it takes you there and back again like Bilbo; but you never return to exactly the same place but to a different turn of the spiral.

The caers are symbols for the three pairs of chakras, the three cauldrons; the roads between them symbolise the threads that link the chakras. Elen's roads are the *song lines* that carry the energies of Life and Love and Light throughout the land, the energies of Warmth and Vocation and Wisdom ... the energies of the Triskele. They carry them through our bodies; they carry them through the Earth's body.

As you wander through the mythologies of the world you find similar concepts everywhere. Carlos Castaneda saw them as the web that makes our bodies and those of all living things, including the Earth. The Northern tradition calls this the wyrd. The Australian peoples see it as song-lines. Watkins saw the Threads as Ley Lines. Hamish Miller saw them as Dragon Lines. Hamish Miller and Paul Broadhurst called them the Michael/Mary lines, recognising their duality and that they carried the masculine and feminine energy, twin spiral lines that twined together, double-helix spirals like that of DNA. In the east the lines are known as meridians and nadis, again *threads* that carry the energy throughout the body.

The lines are, in fact, triple like the *caduceus* staff, with the two snakes twining in opposite directions up the vertical axis ... back to 3-ness again. The triple lines carry the energies of Elen's three caers, connecting everything to everything.

Elen's roads, pathways, within the earth connect the sacred sites, and they are within our bodies too. They, and the spinning wheels of the chakras, are in all living things. Our British ancestors knew this; they knew and walked the energy lines of the antlered reindeer goddess, the most ancient goddess of our land.

Arianrhod

Arianrhod's name means Silver Wheel. It comes from the Welsh *arian*, "silver," and *rhod* comes from the Indo-European root meaning wheel; her name is likely cognate with Proto-Celtic Arganto-rotā, meaning silver wheel.

It's sometimes thought Arianrhod's name may have also been Arianrath; in Irish, *ráth* means earthen ring-fort; this takes us back again to Elen's caers.

The Sanskrit word chakra also means wheel, sometimes fiery wheel. For those who can see, chakras often look like fiery wheels.

Spinning Wheel – Spinning Tower – World Tree Pole

Arianrhod is lady of the spinning tower and of the silver wheel.

This reminded me of Light ... is light particle or waves? Actually it's both.

Light can be labelled with a wavelength, a frequency; it can reflect, refract, interfere, and diffract. In those and other respects, light behaves like a wave.

But light also has a certain amount of energy depending upon its frequency, and it also has momentum. In those respects, it acts like a particle. Some scientists talk about *particle-wave duality*; others even use the word *wavicle*. Being a particle and a wave is not mutually exclusive – the *and/and* principle again; quantum mechanics has reinforced this idea, based on tiny pieces of matter which act as waves.

Arianrhod in her aspect of spinning wheel appears as one thing; in her aspect as spinning tower she appears as another; she is not either/or but and/and.

Lady of the Silver Wheel

The silver wheel is so very similar to the meaning and concept of the Sanskrit word chakra. It is like the seething pool of the *coire* – the Gaelic word for the Cauldrons of Poesy that also means kettle, boiler, vat, dell and whirlpool. Coire is like *chur* in German and *cirque* in French, words that are about amphitheatre-like valleys. One of the very few Celtic words to be borrowed into English is *corrie* which, along with *cwm*, means just the same sort of valley as coire. In the Scottish mountains there are many places with the name coire such as Coire An t-Sneachda (Corrie of the Snows) on Cairngorm; the name defines a circular hanging valley on a mountain; like Elen's *caers,* which are fortresses on hills rather than hanging valleys, they still carry the grail-cup connection.

So Arianrhod carries this grail-concept too.

The cup, grail and cauldron are all similar to the wheel-concept; they all carry the energy of the horizontal axis, the energy of the four elements, of Middleworld. These three pictures of world-tree concepts show Middleworld centred around the trunk of the world tree.

World Trees

The world turns, the four seasons turn and turn about, giving a continuity to Life although no two seasons are ever the same. The horizontal axis also holds the directions – north, east, south, west – that enable us to find our way around the Earth. We live our everyday lives on the wheel, even the day itself is made up of dawn, midday, dusk, midnight.

Arianrhod's silver wheel carries these concepts for us, as do all spirit-wheels in shamanic traditions the world over.

Lady of the Spinning Tower

As Lady of the Spinning Tower, Arianrhod holds the vertical axis of the world tree for us.

In the Celtic tradition a tree or pole is seen as standing at the centre of all things, reaching up into the sky and down into the underworld; again the three pictures show this. Shamans use this pole to climb up to the inspiration of Upperworld or descend into the realms of the Ancestors in Lowerworld. They also use it as a jumping off point for reaching out into Middleworld and the everyday world; the Spinning Tower, Caer Sidhe, spins around to open its gate to the different points of the wheel of the year; the shaman steps out of the Tower through this gate into the space-time where they need to be for the journey and the work.

On the vertical axis, the Tower reaches up into the North Star while its caverns are in the heart of the Earth. Around its trunk circles the Middleworld where we and the rest of creation live and move and have our physical and etheric being here on Earth. We climb the world tree when we go out to journey; it is also our way home; like the fireman we can slide back down the trunk of the tree to return home when the journey is done.

The pole is also known as the broom, besom, *gandreigh*, riding pole, stang, staff and hobby horse – all of these are the shaman's horse. Back in the 1950s, as a child playing hobby-hoss in my home village on the edge of Exmoor, I was told that I was riding the horse that would carry me to the lands of the Faer. Nowadays people tend to consider that only the drum is the shaman's horse, perhaps we've got restricted in our ways? The riding-pole, the symbol of the world tree, is also the otherworldly beast that carries us on our journey.

The tower is a form of the world tree, a place of gateways

between worlds. There are many doors that will take you to different space-times, different worlds as well as different times and places on the Earth. Lots of patience, time and practice is needed to learn how to do this and exploring the Celtic chakra system is a very good way to begin.

As we learn to work with the chakras we come to realise that each chakra is made up of *both* the silver wheel *and* the spinning tower; the vertical and horizontal axes that hold the two energies of the receptive and the creative ... the queen and king again.

We can travel up and down the vertical axis of each chakra to step out onto the horizontal axis to journey. The vertical tower axis becomes our own personal riding-pole as well as the axis upon which the Earth spins.

Spinning Serpent

6-armed cross

The chakra, in the Celtic system has a basic structure or skeleton; I call it the 6-armed cross. In the Norse tradition the rune that looks like this is called *Jor* or *Ior* and is the rune of the Midguard Serpent who is called Jormungandr.

Jormungandr is about liminal spaces, being between worlds; about union, synthesis and uniting opposites, and about seeing all sides of something. Jor is also an excellent bind-rune for wards and blocks. The chakra is about all of these are things too. Each chakra, and the whole system, both is and defines a liminal space. The word liminality comes from the Latin word *līmen* meaning threshold; it is about being on the "threshold" of or between two different existential planes. Writers such as Arnold van Gennep and Victor Turner have used the term in their anthropological theories of ritual and rites of passage. Liminal beings are often Tricksters; their role is to challenge you as you try to pass them, trick you off your path, generally see if you are up to it for your initiation. Dragons – as Jung knew well – and serpents are often the form such tricksters take in western traditions. Jung said of the Unconscious, *"here be your dragons, guarding your treasure"*; he implied that they guarded it from ourselves until such time as we are able to work appropriately with it.

Jormungandr is such a serpent. S/he – for this serpent carries both genders – holds and guards the skeleton-structure of the world tree. S/he challenges us on both our going out and our coming home; when we go to find our way in to explore and learn … and then when we come to find our way out again to share our wisdom with the world.

To way of the chakras is by no means a rose-strewn path, it is follow a way full of challenges. Arianrhod's spinning tower is hard for us to enter, then hard for us to leave; it is a liminal place, a threshold of consciousness as well as a threshold between worlds. Her silver wheel is another challenge; being silver, it mirrors us back to ourselves and flashes tricksy images into our mind's eye that can easily confuse … what is real and what is not? And what is reality anyway? All these are questions Arianrhod asks us and she is no sweetness-and-light lady but a formidable teacher; we get no quarter in her tower.

Arianrhod's tower is also called Caer Sidi, the Glass Castle or Spiral Tower and is traditionally the place wherein lore keepers serve their apprenticeship. The terms are strict and it is thought of as imprisonment. In the Celtic stories many folk (including Arthur) are imprisoned there, or perhaps one should say they get stuck there until they learn how to emerge. Taliesin says that he spent three periods in the prison of Arianrhod, learning his trade of seer and poet – the art of seeing clearly (clairvoyance) and the art of telling well so his audience could learn too (poetry); two basic skills for the shaman. Thomas of Erceldoune, the Scottish shaman or *taibhsear* (pronounced tah-shar) also spent seven years in the tower, in the land of the queen of Efland, as his story-song tells us, and came out with the silver tongue and the ability to see clear.

Taliesin's apprenticeship actually begins with Ceridwen – I tell the story in her chapter – where he is chased through the four elements of the silver wheel, eaten and reborn. At the beginning of his story he is known as Gwion Bach, only after he is reborn again, out of the leather bag floating in the river, is he given his bardic name of Taliesin which means Shining Brow. This takes us to the idea of the brow chakra, where all the threads from the three pairs of chakras are integrated, another part of Arianrhod's realm.

Lady of the Moon & Stars

As Lady of the Moon and Stars, Arianrhod holds the energy of the sky-starways and the earth-starways as well as the moonpaths. The stars in the sky link with the crystal stars of the Earth making energy threads which connect our planet with all the rest of the stars and planets in our solar system. Our galaxy and the whole of the cosmos are within her purview; within her range of vision and understanding and insight, her outlook and experience.

Arianrhod is a teacher and tester; she hones our spirit, helps us to keep our lens clean and bright. As George Bernard Shaw said …

Better keep yourself clean and bright. You are the window through which you must see the world.

Dag Hammarskjold also has a useful quote for this …

You are the lens in the beam. You can only receive, give, and possess the light as the lens does. If you seek yourself, you rob the lens of its transparency. You will know life and be acknowledged by it according to your degree of transparency, your capacity, that is, to vanish as an end, and remain purely as a means.

I love this quote; it shows us how to be unselfish and inclusive, useful to our fellow creatures. I wish more of us could see and comprehend it rather than always searching for ourselves, putting ourselves first.

Caer Arianrhod's labyrinthine turnings offer us the wisdom, from following the spiralling path through the chakras, to find our raison d'etre, our job description for the incarnation and some hints at least of the great plan behind that.

A good mantram to use on this journey is the Affirmation of the Disciple ...

I am a point of light within a greater light,
I am a strand of loving energy within the stream of love divine,
I am a point of sacrificial fire focused within the fiery heart of god,
And thus I stand.
I am a way by which men may achieve,
I am a source of strength enabling them to stand,
I am a beam of light shining upon the way,
And thus I stand.
And standing thus revolve
And tread this way the ways of men,
And know the ways of god,
And thus I stand.

The Northern Lights

Arianrhod's caer is the constellation called the corona borealis, the Crown of the North. She also shows herself to us as the wonderful phenomenon we know as the Northern Lights. If you ever get the opportunity to go see the Lights do take it; they are quite amazing. The old traditions are still extant among the Sami folk who follow the reindeer – Elen of the Ways totem beast. There, in the north, they say you should speak to the lights, *ask* them to come and show themselves to you and offer a gift. You never command or try to trick the lights. Offering a gift is a fundamental shamanic concept throughout the world and very strong in the Celtic tradition – the offer of exchange; it's respectful; it acknowledges and accepts your relationship with otherworld and with the lady of the aurora borealis, whose northern "crown of light" it is. You always offer an exchange in any work you do with Otherworld.

The chakras are places of transformation and transmutation, places of spinning, weaving energies (like the aurora borealis) that spin between the worlds.

Journey: Northern Lights

The Northern Lights ...

Find yourself at the North Pole; blue whiteness all around you; stillness ... is that the stars themselves you can hear singing?

You are alone, only yourself for company; this is good but, at the same time, you would like someone to share the amazing sense of joy that is welling up inside you.

At the very edge of sound you hear, behind you, the slightest crunch of the top-crust of snow.

You don't turn round but your heart is full of hope.

Soft, warm breath strokes the back of your neck; all the hairs rise but still you don't turn.

'Who are you?' you whisper.

The breath caresses your neck again but no-one speaks.

'Who are you?' you say again.

Again, the breath warms you.

'Who are you?' you ask for the third time.

A rough, soft tongue gently licks the back of your neck.

Now you do turn.

There, glimmering silverly against the night-snow is a polar bear. She is huge; her great white paws hardly sink into the crust of snow, each one is as big as your head.

And yet you are not frightened; you can feel the warmth coming from the aura you just now realise you are seeing around her. Her aura shimmers and swings about her like a curtain of light. Her eyes are like dark pools of night but there, in their depths, stars shine.

You are entranced by her eyes, feeling yourself twining with her spirit. As you feel this you realise a smile is beginning on those great jaws.

'Yes,' you hear inside your head, 'yes, it is I.'

And suddenly you know that you are in the presence of the Snow Queen herself, Arianrhod, lady of the Moon and Stars. You greet her.

'Come with me,' she tells you.

She curls you into her great front paws; you feel like one of her cubs, with Mother, sat learning the ways of Earth.

Wrapped in her warm fur, safe in her arms, you accompany Arianrhod as she carries your spirit up into the sky. There, all around you, hang great curtains of light, all the colours of the rainbow shimmering iridescent in the velvet-black sky. They are curtains of fire, cold ice-fire flickering across the millions of miles of space.

'This is my home,' you hear in your head, 'my temenos; the womb of darkness from which all life is born; all life and all ideas.'

It is a liminal space, a threshold, you see and sense that. Now, with Arianrhod as the great white Mother Bear, you are able to stand at this threshold. One day, you will cross it, when you are able, when you are ready. On that day you will follow Arianrhod through the curtains of light and know the greater universe ... and, following Arianrhod, you will return, cross back again through the curtains of light, to bring what you know back to your own folk.

As you realise this you find yourself again sat in the arms of the Mother, the great polar bear, cradled at the top of the world, in the blue-white snow, the dark velvet sky above you spangled with diamond-stars and the rainbow-curtains of light and fire and ice shimmering and flickering all around.

'They are my crown,' Arianrhod tells you, 'the Aurora Borealis. I am Queen of the North.'

You know this; suddenly you find you know all sorts of things although you don't yet have words for many of them. Her words, queen of the north, remind you of Arthurian tales; a whole flood of memory falls around you, like the curtains of light, but you know better than to chase those rainbows now … later, there will be time later to absorb it all.

'Help me to remember,' you ask Arianrhod.

A soft, deep growl answers you, almost like a huge purr.

'It is time for you to go, little one,' Arianrhod tells you, motherly.

Reluctantly you realise this is so.

'Thank you, Mother,' you tell her. 'I will come back – if I may? I would learn with you again.'

The soft-rough tongue touches your forehead, warm breath surrounds you; you shut your eyes.

When you open them again you are back in your own world, in your own space, in your everyday body. You stay still, don't move, allowing the feelings to well up through you; there may be sadness and longing to return as well as the joy, let them all flow through you, sit quiet and allow the light and the dark to move through you, filling you with a new sense of knowing.

When you are ready, take a deep breath and sigh it out, take another and sigh that out too, and a third. Swallow, move your mouth, wiggle your fingers and toes, rub your hands together then rub your knees and legs and arms, have a good stretch and a yawn, then open your eyes. Blink a few times, move your head gently on your neck, hunch your shoulders and let go, rub your feet on the floor. When you feel that you're safely back in your body thank your body for being there for you to return to.

Make notes and drawings to remind you of your journey then make yourself a warm drink and have something nice to snack on. You have done a lot of work so you need to replenish your body for the energy it gave you while you worked – exchange again.

Ceridwen & the Cauldrons of Poesy

The Cauldrons of Poesy are another way in which the chakras are shown in the Celtic tradition. The earliest written reference to the cauldrons is in a poem in a 16th century manuscript, containing glosses that date back to the 11th century, however the poem goes way back beyond that. It is attributed to Amergin who was a similar poet-teacher to Taliesin in the Gaelic tradition.

Taliesin was initiated by Ceridwen. His story, very briefly, is that Ceridwen needed him to stir her cauldron for a year and a day; she was making an elixir that would give her son, Dark Crow, all the wisdom of the universe. Taliesin (then called Gwion Bach) stirred dutifully until, on the very last day, the cauldron began to bubble and spat three boiling drops of liquid onto his thumb. It hurt! Taliesin stuck his thumb in his mouth and consequently got the wisdom intended for Ceridwen's son. He realised this and ran, scared the goddess would have him for breakfast for taking the wisdom from her son. Ceridwen chased after him. Gwion ran and ran, terrified out of his wits, and suddenly found he had become a hare, running and leaping over the ground. Then he heard the barking behind him and realised Ceridwen had become a greyhound, snapping at his heels. He leapt into the air and came down in the river. He swam and swam, as fast as he could go, then he heard behind him the sound of an otter swimming even faster and catching up with him. He put on a spurt and found he had become a salmon. He made it to the weir and, leaping in his salmon-shape, he tried to get up the weir. Three times he tried and, on the third try, he flapped his fins desperately trying get over the fall … and found he had become a pigeon. The pigeon is a wonderful flyer, very fast and nimble, so Gwion did his best to fly as fast as he could. Then, overhead he heard the scream of a peregrine falcon. Gwion thought all was lost. He shut his eyes and his wings and dropped like a stone out of the sky … to find he had landed in a pile of wheat, had indeed become a grain of wheat. He kept as still as he could, not thinking of anything, and then he heard it. Prrrk, prrk, prk ... the sound of a chiken hunting for food. Ceridwen had become a black hen and was still hunting him. She quickly found him and gobbled him up.

Shifted back into her own form, Ceridwen knew she was pregnant. In nine months she gave birth to a beautiful boy-child. She knew she couldn't keep him so she sewed him into a leather bag and put him in the river. The bag floated downstream until it came to the weir where it bumped and shuffled against the stones. That evening a local prince came down to hunt salmon and found the bag. He opened it up and there was the most beautiful boy-child in the whole world. The prince called him Shining Brow which, in the old tongue, is Taliesin.

Taliesin and Ceridwen are deeply entwined for she enables him to be initiated. The chase, through the four elements – hare/earth, salmon/water, pigeon/air, seed/fire – is a standard initiation test amongst the Celtic peoples; and so is being eaten in order to be reborn. The goddess takes you within and then births you anew, with the wisdom.

As you see Ceridwen is Lady of the Cauldron. She has several of them and they do different things but they are most famous for being places of rebirth – alchemical flasks. This is another of the functions of the chakras.

The Cauldrons of Poesy

Gaelic poem, the Cauldrons of Poesy, by Amergin mac Ecchit (the second Irish Amergin) is a long and complicated piece that can be very hard to understand. I began working with it, and teasing its meanings out, in the late 1980s. It outlines three cauldrons that are *"born to every man"*. They are ...

Cauldron of VOCATION, called Coire Ernmae in Gaelic

Cauldron of WISDOM, called Coire Sois in Gaelic

Cauldron of WARMING, called Coire Goiriath in Gaelic

My work with the Cauldrons of Poesy showed me how they are very similar to the three Taoist cauldrons. They relate to the three pairs of chakras in a similar way to the "triple-heater" symbolism of eastern tradition, determining overall health of the body, emotions, mind and spirit, i.e. how you are evolving spiritually – the four elements and directions again. Wisdom passes everywhere, as the old saying goes. After lots of work and journeying, reading ageless wisdom about chakras, energy centres and cauldrons from all over the world, and digesting it, I realised that the following correspondences make sense.

WARMING	VOCATION	WISDOM
Crown/Base	Heart/Solar Plexus	Throat/Sacral
Smith	Healer	Poet
Strength/Good	Beauty	Wisdom/Truth
Power	Love	Light
Upperworld	Middleworld	Lowerworld
Maiden	Mother	Crone
Red Cup of Lordship	White Cup of Fostering	Black Cup of Forgetfulness
Light colours ... Red	Blue	Green
Life	Consciousness	Wisdom

The Cauldrons of **Vocation** and **Wisdom** need to be turned, each lifetime, to come to their upright positions in order to be filled. The shaman evolves, until she or he becomes able to *consciously* contain the spirit. This means that each pair of chakras becomes integrated, the the shaman finds the "driving seat" in the Brow and sits there; then both knowledge and wisdom can be utilised.

The Cauldron of **Warming** is different; it's the life-carrier and MUST be upright or you would be dead. There's no need to turn this one but it can tip sideways if you're ill.

The cauldrons' positions show the shaman's state of *knowing* as opposed to knowledge, their wisdom, meaning their ability to use what they know in an appropriate way and for the good of others beyond themselves.

no knowing = upside down
half knowing = half-way upright
full knowing = right way up

The Cauldron of Vocation

This cauldron holds the HEART/SOLAR-PLEXUS pair of chakras and is located in the chest, at the heart. It is inverted in people who do not yet aspire to journey on the Path.

It can also be turned sideways or upside-down, from an upright position, by both joy and sorrow as these feelings can cause us to lose our equilibrium. This is not always a bad thing. To experience this cauldron out of alignment can be very enlightening and often helps us realize things. It's good to learn to sit on your hands when things go wrong; never be too eager to turn your own, or someone else's, cauldron right way up, you could slow down or stop the process ... and so the progress!

As a person grows so their cauldron of Vocation turns on its side. This happens as they begin to see something beyond the everyday and, more especially, beyond themselves, and begin to want it. It's important to *want* it this. You have to want; you have to have desire, or you will stay in the same old rut forever.

Desire is *e-motion* ... that which enables motion, just think where you would be without it.

So the cauldron of VOCATION turns through the DESIRE *to know*.

When we set our foot on the Path the cauldron begins to turn. Once it gets half way round *knowing* can begin to stick in it, not fall out, and this tips the balance further. The cauldron swings more upright; this is a process which can happen really slowly so you hardly notice, or it can be very quick (an aha moment), or anything in between.

Once the Cauldron of Vocation begins to turn the Cauldron of

Wisdom also starts to turn and fill. We need the *Path of the Heart* (vocation) in order to achieve the *Path of Wisdom*. The path of the heart is about commitment, committing ourselves to working with otherworld, not just putting our own interests first. Once we begin to think beyond ourselves we can get a deeper and broader view of our place in the general scheme, see how our actions affect everything else and so learn to be care-full. This is the healer's task, learning how and when to care.

The Cauldron of Wisdom

The Cauldron of Wisdom is our own personal *Well of Segais* with our own echo of the salmon of wisdom and ring of hazel trees on which to feed to gain that wisdom.

This cauldron holds the THROAT/SACRAL pair of chakras and is located in the **Throat** chakra (NOT the crown as is often thought). This cauldron is upside down until we begin to learn wisdom – as opposed to learning and knowledge. Wisdom is not knowledge, although it uses knowledge in its functioning; think about that, it's important not to confuse wisdom/knowing (kenning in the old tongue) with knowledge. Wisdom is about knowing *how and when to use* knowledge and about when to refrain from using it and sit on your hands ... a vital skill for the shaman.

You need to fill your *library-of-being* with all the *books-of-experience* you can manage; then you need to brew all that in the cauldron for a year-and-a-day in order that the cauldron will boil and spit the three drops of wisdom onto your thumb so you can suck them up. Having alphabet soup after your name tells people you're an incredible swot ... it does *not* tell them you have the foggiest clue what to do with all that knowledge. Knowledge can be a burden, fogging your vision with preconceptions and perceived wisdom so you have no room to *know* (to ken) anything; it can be a millstone round your neck ... or stepping stones on your path to wisdom. Wisdom is about discerning what is baby and what is bathwater ... and only throwing out the one you don't need. This is the poet's task, the wisdom keeper and the cyfarwydd who tells the wisdom on to enable the people.

As you gain some wisdom so the cauldron gradually tips and moves, turns. When you have the knack of wisdom then the cauldron turns right side up and you can fill it easily.

Ponder on all this and begin to make it your own, taking it into your *knowing* of the chakras. The traditions of our Earth have differing stories, differing terminology, but her wisdom is all the same. Part of our job is to assimilate this wisdom and make it a part of ourselves. Another part is to real-ise – make real and show – the wisdom and give it back to our people.

The Cauldron of Warming

This cauldron is the well-spring and source of life in each of us. It holds the life-thread without which we cannot exist in incarnation. The life-thread connects us here and is withdrawn from here when we die.

It holds the CROWN/BASE pair of chakras and is located in the Crown. It is also called the "cave in the head" and is sometimes seen as a halo, as shown in mediaeval pictures; it is the source of the "light in the head" which people see as they progress along the path.

The cauldron is upright at birth and, barring sickness when it may tip sideways, remains so throughout our lives.

The Cauldron of Warming is the source of energy that maintains our lives; it is warmed by the breath of the soul and empowered by the vitality of the blood thus connecting us to both Spirit and Earth.

It holds the fires of *vitality* and the enabling power which sustains our activity in the three worlds; these are echoed in the Base chakra and felt there quite strongly. This cauldron turns upside down at death. As you develop etheric vision you are able to see this, to actually see the cauldron turn upside down as someone dies.

Meet the Three Cauldrons

Preparation

Choose a suitable time to do the journey.

Do this ritual for three days before your journey, at both morning and evening *twilight* or as near to this as you can.

EARTH – Take a handful of soil from your own garden/ window box/plant pot. Thank the soil for being there and smooth it gently onto your face; leave it there until the ritual is completed.

WATER – Hold a glass or small bowl of water in your hands. Thank the water for being there and drink from it. Keep the rest of the water for the ending of the ritual.

AIR – Light a small piece of incense, smell and watch the smoke rising into the air. Thank it for being there.

FIRE – Light a candle. Feel the warmth and see the light; look into the heart of the flame and thank it for being there.

ENDING – Wash the earth from your face with the water from the glass or bowl. Rub your hands dry in the smoke of the incense and then douse the incense. Blow out the flame of the candle and as you do so watch the smoke disappear and let it carry these words, aloud, into Otherworld *"I journey to meet the three cauldrons."*

After doing your ritual each time make sure you clean up the space. Remember, SILENCE is the watch-word – do NOT tell your experience abroad, hold it sacred and secret within yourself, allow it space and time to gestate else you will abort it or give it premature birth.

Journey: Meet the Cauldrons

This is a journey through your own chakras, to meet the Cauldrons.

- PREPARE YOUR SPACE – physical cleaning and setting up your altar.
- COVER YOUR EYES
- NOW – LIE STILL. *Feel* your breathing. Don't try to change anything.
- Find yourself in your sacred space, be at home there.
- When you are ready, go out ...
- See a pathway, a thread of light, shimmering and spinning out before you, leading you to the CAULDRON OF VOCATION.
- Follow the path ...

NOW ... move your *focus* and your *consciousness* to sit beside the CAULDRON OF VOCATION. Settle your consciousness quietly there.

Ask the Cauldron of Vocation to show you itself; its two sides – the Heart and the Solar Plexus – and to show you the thread, the pathway, between the two. This pathway goes in both directions, both widdershins and deosil, from heart to the solar plexus *and* from the solar plexus to the heart. Everything always goes in both directions ... that ability (there and back again as Bilbo puts it) is a function of the enabling, empowering current of duality.

When you are ready, thank the Cauldron of Vocation for all it has given you and say you will return to learn more.

Now – see a pathway, a thread of light, shimmering and spinning out before you from the Cauldron of Vocation, leading you to the CAULDRON OF WISDOM.

Again ... Follow the path ...

Move your *focus* and your *consciousness* to beside CAULDRON OF WISDOM. Settle your consciousness there.

Now – ask the Cauldron of Wisdom to show you itself; its two sides – the Throat and the Sacral – and to show you the pathway between the two. Again, this pathway goes in both directions, as do all paths.

When you are ready, thank the Cauldron of Wisdom for all it has given you and say you will return to learn more.

Now – See a pathway, a thread of light, shimmering and spinning out before you from the Cauldron of Wisdom, leading you to the CAULDRON OF WARMTH.

Again … Follow the path …

Move your *focus* **and your** *consciousness* **up to the** CAULDRON OF WARMTH. Settle your consciousness there.

Ask the Cauldron of Warmth to show you itself; its two sides – the Crown and the Base – and to show you the pathway between the two. This pathway too goes in both directions, as all paths do.

When you are ready, thank the Cauldron of Warmth for all it has given you and say you will return to learn more.

Now – See a pathway, a thread of light, shimmering and spinning out before you from the Cauldron of Warmth into the BROW.

Follow the path – **move your** *focus* **and your** *consciousness* to the BROW centre.

Settle your consciousness there. Spend a moment in the bright darkness.

Sense the threads of light going out from the Brow centre to the …

> Cauldron of Vocation that contains the Heart and Solar Plexus.
> Cauldron of Wisdom that contains Throat and Sacral.
> Cauldron of Warmth that contains the Crown and Base chakras.

And see the threads returning from each tower back to the BROW.

When you are ready, thank the Cauldrons and say you will visit again, to learn.

When you are ready, find yourself in your own space back in the everyday world. Greet your body. Thank it for being there for you. Spend time reflecting on what you have been shown. Gently sit up. Make drawings and notes.

When you have finished, clear your space.

Don't forget to eat and drink to replace physical energy and anchor yourself in your body.

Follow-up

Do this ritual for three days after your journey, at both morning and evening *twilight* or as near to this as you can.

EARTH – Take a handful of Earth from your own garden/ window box/plant pot. Thank it for being there, smooth it gently on your face, leave it there until the ritual is completed.

WATER – Hold a glass or small bowl of water in your hands. Thank it for being there and drink from it. Keep the rest of the water for the ending of the ritual.

AIR – Light a small piece of incense, an inch of joss stick perhaps, smell and watch the smoke rising into the air. Thank it for being there.

FIRE – Light a candle. Look into the heart of the flame and thank it for being there.

ENDING – Wash the earth from your face with the water from the glass or bowl. Rub your hands dry in the smoke of the incense and then douse the incense. Blow out the flame of the candle and as you do so watch the smoke disappear and let it carry these words, aloud, into Otherworld *"I have journeyed to meet the Three Cauldrons. I will remember and grow."*

After doing your ritual each time make sure you clean up the space. Remember, SILENCE is the watch-word – do NOT tell your experience abroad, hold it sacred and secret within yourself, allow it space and time to gestate else you will abort it or give it premature birth.

Preiddeu Annwfn: Arthur's Raid on the Underworld

This 9th century Welsh poem is the earliest known story of Arthur; Caitlin & John Matthews have written a good book on Arthur's quest to bring back the cauldron from the Sleeping Lord; but, as well as that, it is also a story about discovering and learning the chakras.

The poem, the Raid on the Underworld, is attributed to the 6th century poet and shaman Taliesin; it's one of the oldest and most enigmatic documents relating to Arthur that we still possess. Within the 61 lines are clues to the Celtic traditions including the chakras.

Arthur and his comrades go down into Annwfn on the ship Prydwen. The name Annwfn means "in-world" and that is worth thinking about. It takes me again to Jung and what he called the unconscious, a place within ourselves that we don't yet know and where our treasure is hidden. The story goes that Arthur heads for the in-world to steal the wonder-working cauldron from the Lord of Annwfn. In many shamanic traditions the concept of "stealing" from the master is very strong and a vital part of the apprentice's training. If we only consider this with our 21st century minds then we are likely to be shocked; if we let go of preconceived ideas and journey on the concept of "stealing from the master" then we will expand our knowing.

In shamanic initiations the "stealing" is a test, of ourselves; do we have the *nous* and the *gumption* to get past the master's wards and take the treasure? A good shaman hopes his apprentices will be quick and sharp and bright enough to do just that; then he will have succeeded not only in teaching them all she or he knows but in enabling them to be better than she is … evolution.

So, Arthur, as "once and future king" sets off with companions to pass his initiation test.

The cauldron Annwfn is guarded by nine maidens whose breath warms the brew. These are the keepers of inspiration, the British muses. The ancient Greek word from which our word "muse" comes may well have grown out of the Proto-Indo-European root-word "mens" which means "to think"; however the thinking referred to is a lot deeper than our ordinary, everyday usage of the word. Taking this on board, our *muse* is the one who helps us to think, ponder, consider, learn and so come to *know*. A cauldron that is breathed into life by nine such beings must be quite something.

Then there are the seven Caers or Towers which the ship, the Prydwen, sails past. Each caer has its own secrets, the secrets of the chakras whose energy it holds and each one is protected by warriors who defend its energy – we will be talking about them shortly, they are a fundamental part of the chakra system both east and west.

Arthur journeys with *three* ship-loads of men packed into his vessel. Again, this pinged off lots of light bulbs inside my head when I read it: I got the connections – the three pairs of chakras, each having their guardian-warriors. His vessel is both the physical thing and the symbol for his self; the incarnate self is often called the *vessel* in esoteric work and this is certainly esoteric work. Esoteric means obscure, mysterious, abstruse, impenetrable, cryptic, arcane, secret, occult; the Celtic stories, like most mystery traditions, are certainly all of these!

The warriors help to make sure of this too. Earlier we spoke of the shamanic significance of stealing, how the master hopes the student will find their way through the labyrinth, past the wards and to the treasure. The warriors hold the same signifi-cance as dragons guarding our treasure or all the other things we learn about in faerie stories (lore and grammarye stories). We have to find our way with the warriors. Arthur's story doesn't say anything about this; it is a 9th century copy of a 6th century poem, copied by a monk who was of the new rather than the old ways and may not have had sympathy with them. It's likely some of the original lore-story got lost in the years between.

These are the first five verses of the poem. I've done this as a table so you can see the seven caers Arthur passes; his work at each caer is hardly detailed at all although hints are given.

I praise the Sovereign, High Prince of the kingly land,	1. Caer Sidi
Who encompasses the margins of the world.	
Gweir's captivity in Caer Sidi was resonant	
With the tale of Pwyll and Pryderi.	
None before him was sent into it,	
Into the heavy blue chain that bound the faithful youth.	
Because of the raid upon Annwfn he sorely sang.	
Until the world's ending our poet's prayer shall sound:	
Three ship-burdens of Prydwen entered within;	
Except seven, none rose up from Caer SIDI.	

I am renowned in fame: the song was heard	2. Caer Feddwit
In Caer Pedryfan, four times revolving.	
My original song stems from the cauldron,	
By the breath of nine maidens was it kindled.	
The Chief of Annwfn's cauldron, what is its power?	
Ridged with enamel, rimmed with pearl,	
It will not boil the coward's portion, it is not destined.	
The sword of Lleawc flashed before it	
And in the hand of Lleminawc was it wielded.	
Before hell's gate lights were burning.	
When with Arthur we went to the harrowing.	
Except seven none rose up from Caer FEDDWIT.	

I am renowned in fame: the song was heard 　　　3. Caer Rigor
In the four-square fort, in the Island of the Flaming Door.
Fresh water and jet are mixed,
Bright wine is the drink served to the host.
Three ship-burdens of Prydwen we took to sea:
Except seven none rose up from Caer RIGOR.

I give no reward to the Lord's book-men 　　　4. Caer Wydyr
Who beyond Caer WYDYR saw not Arthur's valour.

Six thousand men there stood upon the wall, 　　　5. Caer Goludd
Hard it was to parley with their sentinel.
Three ship-burdens of Prydwen we went with Arthur:
Except seven none rose up from CAER GOLUDD.

I give no reward to the clerics with trailing shields, 　　6. Caer Fandwy
Who know not who created who,
Nor the hour when the chick was born,
Who made him, why he went not to the meadows of Defwy.
They know not whose the brindled ox, thick his headband,
With seven score links upon his collar.
When we went with Arthur on arduous visit;
Except seven none rose up from Caer FANDWY.

I give no reward to the clerics of weak intent 　　　7. Caer Ochren
Who know not on what day the Chief was made,
Who do not know the hour of the owner's birth,
Nor what silver-headed beast they guard.
When we went with Arthur, disastrous contention:
Except seven, none rose up from Caer OCHREN.

I've left the last two verses out as they have a different feel (for
me) to the first five. I wonder when they were added and am
extremely suspicious of the last line, "*Christ is my guerdon*"; this

is certainly a Christian monk's addition and would (obviously) have had no place in the ancient lore story which is very much older than Christianity.

Arthur's journey begins at CAER SIDI, Arianrhod's caer, the first caer of his journey. It speaks of the sovereign as a prince but that could either be the monk or the deeper sense of the word prince which is not gender-dependent but is a job description, and was still used as such even into Medieval England – Elizabeth I was described as a puissant prince. The sovereign is of the kingly land – this is how our ancestors (like all shamans) think of the land, the earth, with themselves as the guardian-kings serving their folk. Arthur enters with three ship-burdens; this, for me, strongly suggests allusion to the three pairs of chakras which, at this point in his journey, will not be organised or aligned as they will once he has learned to work with them.

The journey continues to CAER FEDDWIT, the second caer of the journey, which it tells us is sung of in Caer Pedryfan as *four times revolving*. It goes on to tell us that here is the cauldron kindled by the breath of nine maidens. It also tells us that this cauldron will not boil the coward's portion, suggesting we need to have our courage and our confidence up to work with this one. It offers us a sword wielded by Lleawc, for whom it flashed, and by the hand of Lleminawc. We are told that before hell's gate lights were burning. All very enigmatic stuff but journeying with it, asking to see it (almost like watching a film and sometimes like taking part in the action) brings many insights to the mind's eye.

Next is CAER RIGOR. We are told it is a four-square fort; this immediately brings up four-ness, four seasons, four elements, the horizontal axis. Four-square is also about squares and cubes which are so often symbols for the Earth, for grounding, for working in the everyday world of our incarnation. It goes on to say the caer has a flaming door – quite a challenge! – and that fresh water and jet are mixed; water and the beautiful black crystal, jet; then that bright wine is served to drink. This is more symbolism; water is often thought of as white (waterfalls perhaps), the jet is definitely black, and wine is often imagined as red. White, black and red ... the three sacred colours that hold the energy of the three worlds and all they pertain to.

Then on to CAER WYDYR where the poem talks about *the Lord's book-men*, what could they be? It says that beyond this place they did not see Arthur's valour. Books speak of the lore and of the ancestors to me, wisdom keepers and knowledge keepers, a library place.

We go on to CAER GOLUDD. It says six thousand men stood upon the walls ... six? The three pairs of chakras are made up of six individual chakras; this number is followed by four zeros to make the number 6000. Zeros have esoteric as well as mathematical functions; if you add a zero to a number you raise it what is called "an order or magnitude", this is similar to raising it up a plane of consciousness. So, adding three zeros takes a number though three planes of consciousness; the three worlds. The verse tells us it was hard to parley with their sentinel ... I can imagine it might be!

Finally we get to the seventh caer, CAER OCHREN. Taliesin says he gives no reward to the clerics – book-learners all, one thinks – who trail their shields; he says that they know nothing of the hour when the chick was born, nor who made him, nor why he went to the meadows of Defwy. He says the clerics *know not whose was the brindled ox* nor of his thick headband, nor of the seven-score links of his collar. Well ... brindled being red and white, and oxen having black hooves brings me back again to the red-white-black of the Celtic triplicity; oxen being of the cow family takes me to Brighid whose totem is the cow and who we visit in another chapter.

The chorus of *'except seven'* comes at the end of each of the first five verses of the poem and is the last line of all; this puts great emphasis on the fact only seven rise up out of each of the seven towers. The poem is deep and mysterious, hard to fathom in the manner of all esoteric lore, all grammarye; to come to know grammarye, how the world and the universe work, requires effort from us. Learning is a journey for each of us with all that that means, as Arthur's journey is in the story. The emphasis on seven, along with all the other hints through Celtic story lore, shows me the chakras. The chakras are fundamental to all life, in all shamanic and later traditions throughout the world, however hidden they may be they are always there. The chakras are part of the framework of the Earth as well as of ourselves and all other life forms. Knowing them is hard work though; we, like Arthur, meet and wrestle (in words, magic and the physical) with other-worldly beings; we journey to strange places, have wild adventures. The voyages are stories, immrama and dreams that run through shamanic traditions offering us clues and hints which, if we follow them, will bring us to truth. The quest is a central part of all shamanic traditions and Annwfn – the in-world – is one of the essential places where we quest.

This story is one of many; Culhwch and Olwen is another which involves travelling through caers, strongholds of wisdom. It's worthwhile following up on all the stores, sitting with them, pondering, allowing their wisdom to seep into you and teasing out the threads of truth.

The cauldron Arthur is hunting in this story is a like the grail and, as we've seen, both grail and cauldron are chakra-symbols in the British tradition. The Celts never confine themselves to one meaning when they can get a whole squadron out of one word, this the poet's skill. The grail is a symbol for each individual chakra *and* for the whole chakra system *and* for the Earth herself, to name just a few things; *and/and* yet again. So a quest for the grail will be a quest for one's own grail *and* the knowing of the chakras as well as for other outer symbols.

The grail-quest, particularly in terms of re-finding the chakras, occurs in every lifetime for us; every time we incarnate we have the opportunity to deepen and broaden our knowing and our knowledge, to increase our awareness another order of magnitude, become more inclusive and find more connections.

The Warriors

In each of the seven towers Arthur goes to there are bands of Warriors defending it. Who and what are they? The poem doesn't tell us, we have to go elsewhere and search around to find our answer.

You may well have heard of or know the prophecy of the Warriors of the Rainbow; the best known version comes from the North American native tradition.

When the Earth is sick and all the animals are dying a tribe of people will come, of all colours and creeds, who will restore the Earth. They will be called Warriors of the Rainbow.

They are also mentioned in the Book of Revelations where it says that *"the number of the saved"* is 144,000.

Representations of the chakras from the east show them as lotus flowers; each flower has the relevant number of petals for its chakra. These "petals" are the Warriors, the individual elements that do the actual work within the chakra.

How 144,000? Each tower has its complement of warriors as follows ...

Chakra	no. of petals/warriors
Crown	x1000
Brow (48 yin + 48 yang petals)	96
Throat	16
Heart	12
Solar Plexus	10
Sacral	6
Base	4
Number of chakra petals within the body	144
Body petals times crown petals	144 x 1000 crown petals
Number of petals in each human (or other) being	144,000

- There are 48 warriors in total in the chakras of the body – base, sacral, solar plexus heart and throat.
- The brow has two petals – looks like a lemniscate – and each of these carries higher levels of the 48 body warriors; one petal carries those with queen-energy, the other carries those with king energy; in the east they call these two energies yin and yang.

So, the body chakras + the brow carry 144 petals ... or warriors.

The crown chakra carries 1000 petal-warriors and is a different kettle of fish to the others as it has the direct connection to other-world. Instead of adding these petal to the others we multiply the others by the 1000 ... this brings us to 144,000, the number of the Rainbow Warriors.

Addition and multiplication have esoteric as well as mathematical significance.

Addition is simple and basic; it takes two or more numbers and adds them together making a *sum* of them: 1+2=3.

Multiplication is a different operation; it gives a *product* rather than a simple sum. It moves the number up a level ... 8 x 10 = 80, for instance. Multiplication moves the 8 one place to the left, it's called up an order of magnitude in maths.

80 x 10 = 800; the 8 has moved two places to the left, up two orders of magnitude.

800 x 10 = 8000; the 8 is now three places to the left, followed by three zeros; has moved up three orders of magnitude.

In the case of the Warriors, the 144 is followed by three zeros and so moves three places to the left; it has moved up *three* orders of magnitude ... three-ness again.

The warriors in the Crown connect directly across the worlds in ways the body and brow warriors do not. Multiplication gives us the sense and realisation of these powers.

This brings us to a different sense of our responsibilities ... the 144,000 warriors are in each of us, they are us. They're not some mythical troupe to which we can aspire to be accepted. They are already there within us, within the chakras which make up each and every one of us.

We all contain the 144,000, the *number of the saved*, the Warriors of the Rainbow, within us. All we have to do is *realise* them, enable them to come alive within us; I say "all we have to do" but it's not an easy thing and can be very scary. It means we each of us have to accept our responsibility for everything we do here on Earth and accept that we have the ability to change things, maybe only in little and only as far as each one of us can go, but the responsibility is to accept that and then to take those little steps. If – no, when – each of us does this we help the world. Think about that in relation to yourself. Each of us is a part of the whole; we can work for the good of that whole, or selfishly for our own good. The latter won't have a lasting or satisfying effect, even for ourselves. The former will automatically mean that we help ourselves at the same time as we work for the good of the whole.

Your journey through this book begins your path of *bringing yourself to* light. Each of us **is** the 144,000 Rainbow Warriors, if and when we choose to realise it and take on our responsibility. We will do just that one lifetime or another. It's about becoming conscious.

It's quite a responsibility to acknowledge, to be part of that which saves the Earth, but that acknowledgement is necessary in order for us to be of use to the Earth. As we all contain the 144,000 warriors – we all have chakras – we are each of us *the number of the saved*; our purpose is to become conscious of this and able to work with it along with working with Otherworld. Are you, when all your warriors are awake and spinning with life within you, willing to be a part of that saviour?

The Native American prophecy fairly well describes the times we are currently living in. Only by being conscious of our place as a vital part of the whole, and that we can, through being conscious, make a difference can we restore the Earth. Our first conscious learning is of how we are made and that we are all made of the same stuff as the rest of creation. Joni Mitchell put it rather well in her song when she said *we are stardust* ... we are indeed and we need to know the Rainbow Warriors within ourselves and work with them for the good of all.

What is a warrior?

Working through the dictionary and the thesaurus offers us many more words than we might have originally associated with the idea of warrior. People tend to stick to one or two translations of a word without exploring further or enlarging their viewpoint. When working with Arianrhod it's much more useful to go outside one's box.

Some of the words I came up with are ...

soldier, fighter, opponent, combatant, challenger, partaker, accomplice, member, contributor, participant, rebel.

Umm! Far more concepts than the basic things most of us probably think of first when we consider the word warrior.

A warrior does all of these things.

Warrior is a challenger. Warrior is one who stretches the imagination, takes you outside of the box. Warrior is an accomplice when you want to go beyond what you know, what your society tells you is "the norm". Warrior is a partaker of the joy and pain of life, exploration and discovery. Warrior is a member of your family, your soul-group, your tribe, your Self; a contributor to the wealth of knowledge and knowing you and your soul-group build up between you. Warrior is a contributor to the pool of knowing of all Life; a participant in Life. And Warrior is a REBEL ... without which everything stagnates.

With this enlarged view of a warrior it's possible to step out on the road of discovery. The spinning towers are the homes of the warriors: they are the CAERS within the body.

The Seats of the Chakras

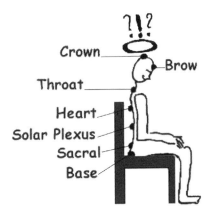

This is a simple exercise but it will help you know yourself, understand things about yourself and begin to learn how to change things within yourself.

The following piece of wisdom may be new to you but KNOWING IT IS IMPORTANT:

- The seats, seeds, essences, spiritual atoms, of each chakra – except the brow – are AT THE BACK of your body, behind the spine, NOT at the front of the body. If your chakras are at the front of your body you will be out of balance and may well feel as if everything is "in your face".
- The BROW is a lemniscate that sits just above and between your eyebrows: its seat is at the front right behind where the two parts of the lemniscate cross.

The journey you're about to do will help you find out where your chakras are; it will also help you begin to learn how to move them towards the spine.

You only need to do this *just a little bit further than is quite comfortable.* Some chakras may go back easier than others or may already be there. Women tend to have trouble getting their heart and solar plexus centres back. Men tend to have trouble with throat and sacral centres.

Journey: where are your chakras seated?

Sit, as in the diagram above, and do the following ...

Get in touch with the warriors of your HEART chakra, see where its seed-atom is situated in your body. If it's not by the spine ask it to move that way – you may need your negotiating skills here as it's probably got into a nice rut and doesn't want to change ... just like you!

When you and HEART have achieved the best compromise possible at this time, assuming it's not yet in the right place, move on to Heart's partner, the SOLAR PLEXUS, and repeat the exercise.

Go next up to the THROAT and ask it to move towards the spine, then move down to Throat's partner, the SACRAL.

Next go up to the CROWN – you should have NO PROBLEMS here! So greet the Crown, see how beautiful it is and move down to Crown's partner, the BASE. You may well have difficulties here; it could be too far back instead of too far forward. Negotiate its return to just behind the spine.

Finally, go to the BROW. If this chakra is *not* just between and in front of your eyebrows you can probably make a mint out of your story; however, you won't be able to do much but look for the time being, so just look – do NOT try to make any changes here, leave it be.

When you are ready to leave, thank all the chakras and say you will visit them again soon to see where they are as you learn more and progress.

Now it is time to come home, to return to the everyday world.

Take a deep breath and sigh it out, take another and sigh that out too, and a third. Swallow, move your mouth, wiggle your fingers and toes, rub your hands together then rub your knees and legs and arms, have a good stretch and a yawn, then open your eyes. Blink a few times, move your head gently on your neck, hunch your shoulders and let go, rub your feet on the floor. When you feel that you're safely back in your body thank your body for being there for you to return to.

Make some notes and drawings to remind you of your journey then make yourself a warm drink and have something nice to snack on. You may not realise it but you've done a lot of work just in that simple-seeming journey and you need to replenish your body for the energy it gave you while you worked … this is exchange again.

Brighid

Brighid is known in the Celtic worlds as Brigantia, Brid, Bride, Briginda, Brigdu, and Brigit. She is goddess of fire and hearth, and of childbirth and inspiration; she is said to lean over every cradle. One of the meanings of her name is Exalted One: her lore and customs continue to this day. Her name in Wales is Fraid.

Three Faces

Brighid has three faces that correspond to the three cauldrons and the three caers. They are ...

SMITH	HEALER	POET
Fire of the Forge	Fire of the Hearth	Fire of Inspiration
Cauldron of Warming	Cauldron of Vocation	Cauldron of Wisdom
Crown/Base	Heart/Solar Plexus	Throat/Sacral
Caer y n'Arfon	Caer Leon	Caerfyrddyn

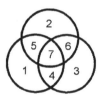 

Central points - Brow Chakra

These diagrams illustrate Brighid's triplicity; in each of them the three circles, points, threads come together at the centre; that centre is the brow chakra. In the first drawing that is shown by the place numbered 7 ... the 7th chakra, the brow chakra.

The brow is the place of integration, of synthesis, where the threads blend; where the three colours of white light – red, blue and green – come together into white light; the synchronised and integrated personality.

What are the Smith, Healer and Poet? These three crafts hold all the things that make up life; they are overlighting job descriptions for each of the three pairs of chakras. The energy of each of these faces, job-descriptions, gives us deeper insight into what each cauldron and caer is about.

I'm using the word *craft* here in talking about each of the faces for the reason that craft is about skills. The thesaurus gives us the following suggestions for the word craft … *ability, artistry, technique, system, practice.* Craft is also about cunning, and cunning folk is what we who follow the old ways call ourselves in Britain. Cunning is about … *wiliness, shrewdness, guile, astute, canny, foxy, smart, perceptive, judicious, incisive, wise, perspicacious, of good judgment* – a host of words that speak of how we are. Note I've included *foxy* for *Fox* is our Trickster-in-Chief, similar to coyote in America, and Tricksters are the very best Teachers in all the worlds, the ones we should learn from most closely.

Smithcraft

Smith – *warming*: blacksmith, maker, forger, creator, fire-worker, iron-worker.

The word Smith comes from an old Teutonic word, *smeithan*, which means to *forge*.

Smithing is about making; smiths are makers.

As blacksmiths, they turn up all the time in songs about the goddess-chase, where the goddess makes her "lover" chase her, if he cannot catch her then she doesn't want him. Two fairly well know such chase songs are the Fith Fath song and the Twa Magicians; despite Victorian romanticism, these are not rape songs but tests, chases set up by the goddess to find a guardain worthy of her. Remember the Troy Town labyrinth chase.

In English the suffix, -*smith*, implies a meaning of specialized craftsmen, for example, wordsmith and tunesmith are synonymous with writer or songwriter, respectively.

The smith is a creator. Smith correlates with the Cauldron of Warming, Caer y n'Arfon and the Crown-Base pair of chakras.

The Crown connects us with otherworld, it is the rainbow bridge between the worlds; our main line back to base. As such it's an information highway for our inspiration ... and for us to send feedback, upload new files we've made from our work-experience here on Earth that will be useful to otherworld. That's a thing about the Celtic tradition; we know information needs to pass in both directions, part of the work is as Ursula le Guin puts it in her novels of the Ekumen, *"The augmentation of the complexity and intensity of the field of intelligent life."* Uploading what we learn and discover in each incarnation helps the whole of otherworld to grow too, nothing stands still.

The Base connects us similarly to the Earth, to the planet on which we have chosen to incarnate and where we have a job; connecting through to our base helps us find out what our job is this lifetime; most of us get a severe dose of spiritual amnesia on being born so we have to work at finding out – a bit like the Swarzneggar film "Total Recall".

Connecting upwards and downwards to Spirit and Earth helps us to do the basic job of being co-creators with otherworld, the job of the Smith.

In Britain, forges were often at crossroads or places where rivers and roads cross; this placing on highways, pathways, has a spiritual connotation as well as an ordinary, everyday obvious ones. On the physical level, business for the smith will be good where there are a lot of travellers; blacksmiths often combined their trade with that of farrier – horse doctor and shoe-smith – so being at a crossroads is a good idea. The paths of Elen of the Ways have crossroads too and their physical counterparts often coincide with our everyday crossroads. Similarly, both Crown and Base chakras are at crossroads between worlds, thresholds, gateways; we can learn to use them as places to exchange wisdom.

Caer y n'Arfon, the fortress and the bridge across the worlds, the cauldron of Warming, will manifests out in the world once we have learned to work with it … with Brighid's help.

Healer craft

Healer – *vocation*: calling, talent, art, passion, foster, nurture, cherish, protect, shelter.

The word Heal is related to the word whole for which the thesaurus offers us *entire, complete, unabridged, intact, unbroken, healthy, sound, fit, well and unity* to expand our ideas about what the word means. It's very much about making whole, bringing together, synthesis, fusion. Curing is *not* really what it's about, nor the concept of "put back together" particularly because of the word "back". There is no return, you can never go back to what was, only to something that looks similar to what you remember; the way, the path, is always forward, onwards. The path forward is always built on the way we have already gone, the past is the rock on which we build the future.

Brighid's face of healer includes the concept of fostering … caring for little ones that are not your own; this is a teaching role, a healer is a teacher in our tradition. Healing in this way is about putting things together and about finding the roots of things.

The Heart connects to our centre, the very centre of the Troy Town labyrinth through which it connects us to the centre of all things. It's about consciousness, the centre of knowing which does not depend on reason or mind-games but *knows* because it is connected to the essence. It is very much about the collecting, inward, centripetal energy that draws all things inwards to itself to bring them together, making whole from the outside in.

The Solar Plexus connects us to the rest of creation all around us, on the horizontal axis, the world guarded by the Midguard Serpent who twines around the trunk of the tree. It spins with the expansive, centrifugal energy that goes outwards, into everything else, linking and joining, making whole from the inside out.

Caer Leon, the place of the flowing waters, the cauldron of Vocation, manifests out in the world once we have learned to work with it ... with Brighid's help.

Wordcraft

Poet – *wisdom*: lore-keeper, history-keeper, ritual-keeper, wordsmith, bard, cyfarwydd

Keeping the word is keeping the lore; we still use the phrase "will you keep your word?" meaning keep your promise. In the old Gaelic ways, the old traditions, the promise was the geis, meaning duty, job and obligation as well as promise. In Welsh we say tynged (plural tynghedau) meaning doom, fate, destiny, similar to some of the concept of wyrd from the Northern tradition. The most famous tynghedau were those that Arianrhod placed on her son Llew Llaw Gyffes.

The poet is both wordsmith, a maker of words, sayings and poems that strike straight through to the heart; and word-keeper, holding the words of the cunning folk and knowing ones of the past and bringing them forward into the present to add to the foundations of the future. She or he carries the songs and stories in the heart and is also able to tell them in a way that moves their listeners, enabling them to journey through the story as well as listen to it.

The Throat is where our voice sings out, it's the wonderful wind-harp that we can learn to use to communicate with others, and not just human others either. It is the instrument of the singer, the taleweaver and even the writer, for good stories when you read them also sing in the ear of the mind. It carries the expansive, outward pouring centrifugal energy that communicates in the world.

The Sacral carries the inward-winding, spiralling centripetal energy of the creative principle. This can appear simply as a new child in the world; it can also appear as wonderful song, picture, statue, poem, story, scientific discovery, mathematical insight, dish of food, piece of technology, philosophical insight ... any creative thing that will reach out to others.

Caerfyrddyn, the sea fortress, the cauldron of Wisdom manifests out in the world once we have learned to work with it ... with Brighid's help.

Brigands & Warriors

Brighid is also patron of warfare (Briga) and her soldiers were called Brigands. Like most old words their origin and meaning is overlaid with centuries of "Chinese whispers"; it seems that we can go back through the Middle English *brigaunt*, from Middle French *brigand*, from Old Italian *brigante*, from *brigare* to fight, from the Celtic *briga* meaning strife and akin to Old Irish *brig* meaning strength. Tossing this word around reminded me of the word *assassin*, coming to us through the legends of the mystery-warriors, the Hashishin, who journeyed with the gods using the sacred weed. They were an order of Nizari Ismailis from Persia and Syria living and working from around 1092 to 1265, and posed a strong military threat to Sunni Saljuq authority within the Persian territories. They captured and inhabited many mountain fortresses under the leadership of Hassan-i Sabbah. Chinese whispers set in again here because, according to texts from Alamut, Hassan-i Sabbah called his disciples Asasiyun, meaning people who are faithful to the Asās, faithful to the 'foundation' of the faith. It's said the word was misunderstood by foreign travellers because it sounded similar to hashish. It just goes to show how we need to think and consider words and their meanings to see if there is more than just what we're given on the surface ... often there is.

I don't know where truth lies for the assassins as I've not journeyed with them. The truth about Brighid and her brigands takes us back to the Rainbow Warriors again. There are, and were, real physical people who were brigands in the current common usage of the word but way, way back if we care to take the journey there are deeper meanings.

TS Eliot put it very well for me – this whole problem about what is real, what is true – when he wrote, in Burnt Norton, *"Humankind cannot bear very much reality"*. We really do need to stretch our boundaries and climb out of our boxes with regard to reality; it's good to learn to bear more reality and realise it may set all our current mores and ideals on their heads ... often this is good thing. Brighid and her brigands do this for me, stretch my boundaries and I really enjoy this, it's like going anew into the Enchanted Forest by a route I've not done before and finding new places.

Warriors, soldiers, brigands ... this takes me to Morris Dancing, one of our ancient customs here in Britain. The Morris traditions get diminished to a manageable size when people think of them only as a bit of fun, a good excuse for downing some nice ale, a way of attracting the girls, etc, etc, but they are far more than that. John Matthews has done some excellent research on the old ways and I remember what I was told when I was a child in my home village on the edge of Exmoor. The cunning folk remember but it's not some "big deal" to us mostly but just "how it is", how life is and a part of us that holds and carries on the continuity of tradition that's been overlooked and diminished in this country for a long time.

Likely you've seem Morris sides dancing, men with bells on their legs, in funny clothes, waving sticks and handkerchiefs; sometimes there's a Beast, Dragon or Fool with them and, around Beltane there may well be a Fair Maid. Old ways that are still carried on now include the Bride; women who marry at this time may well ask the Morris side to come to the wedding to carry them in and out, as the representative of Brighid, for their own wedding. I've done handfastings where this tradition has been included. Who and what are the Morris Men? There's all the usual academic discussion about where the word Morris comes from – Moorish, Mary's men, just to put up a couple of currently perceived pieces of wisdom, both of which have strains of truth within them.

The name Mary has strong Christian connotations nowadays but comes from far older words; one of which is a word for *sea*. Lady of the Sea is an ancient concept, it seems our ancestors knew very well that we came from the sea and (unlike the dolphins) didn't go back to it. It takes us to one of the bases in creation myths and the ultimate in magic – bringing together fire and water – perhaps the best known is the Northern story of fire and ice.

For us, the lady of the sea (water!) wedding the lord of the sun (fire) certainly makes sense of what science tells us too about how life comes about. Our ancestors didn't talk as we do, riddling and story were their way, along with songs; we should not denigrate them because they are not like us, perhaps they were even wiser?

Remembering Elen and Macsen, the goddess and her guardian, we can take another look at Morris Men. The hints and stories suggest to me, as they do to John Matthews, the goddess' band of guardians ... her Brigands and her warriors. I do tai chi; when I got to being able to begin the stick work I was immediately struck by how similar many of the exercises are to the dance moves of a Morris side. Carry this idea on into the work with handkerchiefs and you have a technique of martial arts that can be practiced as dance and, in the dance, is also a commemoration and glorification of the goddess. We dance the goddess, show her how we are able to be her soldiers, guard her, and give her praise and honour too.

You'll not likely find many sides that will talk much to you about this although some may; here in Britain we don't advertise or proselytise, we just get on with it. If you are polite and not pushy, just keep on going to dances, buy the men a beer, chat about dogs or daffodils or something and are generally respectful and amusing then you'll gradually come to see things as you watch; and maybe they'll even talk to you too.

So, Brighid's brigands may well also be in the Morris sides; they'll be in other things too. Another thought from John Matthews is about the Robin Hood connections and the Green Man. The thing everyone remembers about Robin Hood is that he robbed the rich and gave to the poor; we all still love this concept. The idea of brigands may well hold this too; a rebalancing of the resources so everyone has enough. It's interesting to realise that, until farming, there was no concept of land ownership – we were owned by the land, we were the servants of the land. That changed with farming and the loss of the ways (and respect) of the hunter-gatherers. Perhaps the brigands were trying to rebalance this too, to open up Elen's Ways again that had been taken from us by the land-owners and farmers? It's all speculation but wandering paths in this way takes one's head out of the box.

Brighid's warriors, brigands, were said to be inhabitants of mountain places; this brings me back to the idea of caers and mountain corries. Myths all over the world tell of those who live in the mountains; they work in the high places, making contact with the spirits who live and work beyond our Earth; they come down into the everyday world and give us the wisdom they've collected. The shaman's job is to go out across the worlds, gain wisdom and bring it back to their folk.

The chakras and their warriors are like this. We go to the warriors to learn from them and give them our experience (exchange, again), then we bring this wisdom out into our lives and those we touch. It's worth remembering again – from the last chapter – that warrior has meanings beyond our everyday ones … soldier, fighter, opponent, combatant, challenger, partaker, accomplice, member, contributor, participant, rebel. We need to take each of these concepts within us, sit with them and find out how they work with us; then we are working with the warriors.

Brighid and the Brow Chakra

[Fig 15 – to left of next para and list: Brow Chakra]
This diagram expresses how the Brow chakra works very well.

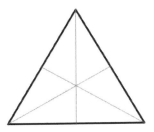

- 6 lines come together at the central point.
- Each of these lines has a different start/end point: one end emerges or finishes from an angle, a corner of the triangle; the other end emerges or finishes at a straight line.
- The angle and the straight line symbolise pairs of opposites that are each one half of the same thing.
- Each of the lines symbolises a Cauldron or caer and the pair of energies it holds.
- The three lines symbolise Elen's ways between the caers, the connecting paths, deer-trods, that we follow to find our way.

The central point is the Brow chakra, where all these pairs of opposites come together.

Brighid shows us this through her three faces that are one face and one being, a synthesis of the whole. When we have spent a long time with the chakras, cauldrons, caers and the ways between them we come to our own knowing of how all the stories show us the many ways of seeing the wonderful web.

67

Journey: Rainbow Dance

Take yourself to the Brow centre.

- Settle yourself quietly there and wait; look around, get a feel for where you are and how this place is appearing to you at this time.
- Find yourself sat in the centre of a wonderful pyramid of light; all the colours of the rainbow play around you in shimmering shadows; they colour you as they flow over you.
- High above you, at the central point of the pyramid, is a sphere of white light spiralling and twisting.
- Out of the spiral flow 6 quicksilver threads.
- 3 go to the corners of the pyramid.
- 3 go to the middle of the long sides between the corners at the base of the pyramid.
- The threads are silvery but, at the same time, they shimmer with all the colours of the rainbow.
- As you sit there, in the middle of the pyramid, it feels like being the May Pole at the centre of the dance.
- 3 of the threads dance around you going widdershins.
- The other 3 threads dance round you deosil.
- They make rainbow patterns on and in you as they dance; you can sense the 6-fold energies of Warming, Vocation and Wisdom spinning through you in both their feminine and masculine forms.
- Enjoy this; allow the threads to caress you, stroke you, dance in you; allow yourself to absorb the energies; don't try to understand or comprehend them yet, just allow them in.
- You may hear music or sound as you are danced by the threads, enjoy and allow this too.
- Gradually, you realise that the dance has ceased.
- The rainbow energies hang shimmering around you and

you, at the centre-pole, are the still-point, the still point where the dance is; the dance is all inside you now.

- Be still with this stillness for a few moments.
- When you are ready to leave, thank the Rainbow energies of the white light in the Brow and say you will visit there again to learn more and enjoy.

Now it is time to come home, to return to the everyday world. Take a deep breath and sigh it out, take another and sigh that out too, and a third. Swallow, move your mouth, wiggle your fingers and toes, rub your hands together then rub your knees and legs and arms, have a good stretch and a yawn, then open your eyes. Blink a few times, move your head gently on your neck, hunch your shoulders and let go, rub your feet on the floor. When you feel that you're safely back in your body thank your body for being there for you to return to.

Make a few notes and drawings to remind you of your journey then make yourself a warm drink and have something nice to snack on. You may not realise it but you've done a lot of work just in that simple-seeming journey and you need to replenish your body for the energy it gave you while you worked.

Summing Up

The chakras are the places where the threads of energy which make up your etheric body meet – a set of Grand Central Stations up your spine.

The chakras are ...

- the towers, caers and castles that hold and guard these Grand Central Stations crossroads or intersections
- the ways between them are Elen's pathways
- they are the cauldrons where the pairs of opposite brew together to create oneness
- they are the seven caers where Arthur learned his way when he journeyed through the In-World
- they are the three faces of Brighid, warmed by the breath of the nine maidens – three times three – that carry the energies of the chakras and bring them all to focus.

The beginning of TS Eliot's poem *Burnt Norton* says so much for me ...

At the still point of the turning world. Neither flesh nor fleshless;
Neither from nor towards; at the still point, there the dance is,
But neither arrest nor movement. And do not call it fixity,
Where past and future are gathered. Neither movement from nor
*   towards,*
Neither ascent nor decline. Except for the point, the still point,
There would be no dance, and there is only the dance.

The Celtic chakra tradition shows us this dance through story, riddle, song, dance; we learn the dances and draw them all together to the centre point, the still point within each of us ... where the dance is.

About Elen Sentier

I was born on Dartmoor in Britain, of a family of cunning folk, awenyddion, spirit keepers and taleweavers following the old ways of this land. I grew up on Exmoor spending much of my free time exploring the moors on foot and horseback learning from the wildwoods, beasts, birds and plants. The patron lady of my home village is the ancient mother-goddess Iwerydd and my aunt used to own her sacred well which gives "clear sight"; cures cataract and gives the ability to see across space-time, what the CIA call far-viewing. The village still does the mummers play on Iwerydd's story, very much Christianised now but the tradition is still alive, and girl children are still sometimes called Urith.

My mother's mother was a witch from the Isle of Mann, my father was a spirit keeper and storyteller. Aunts and uncles worked with herbs and plant and animal spirits, gardening and farming. I spent many nights sat amongst the trees on the edge of Dartmoor, with my uncle, learning from foxes, dormice, weasels, rabbits, badgers and hunting owls, all the night denizens of the wild woods. Uncle could call a wild hawk to his fist and have an adder twine around his wrist. I spent my childhood and youth learning the ways of animals and plants from the ancient traditions handed down through the family and village elders.

My father's family also had very close connections to the theosophists. My grandmother's cousin was Esther Bright a close friend of Annie Besant; Esther's mother, Ursula, was an outstanding worker for women's rights and an active supporter of the Theosophical Society. Ursula donated generously to the building of the Benares (Varanasi) TS Centre and provided a home for Annie Besant when the latter was in England. Ursula was married to the Rt. Hon. Jacob Bright MP who pioneered women's rights with the Married Women's Property Act.

I've done all sorts of things in my current incarnation. I started out teaching Rudolph Laban Modern Educational Dance but went on to do contemporary dance, partly with Robert Cohen at The Place in London. Then I took a big step sideways and joined the Ministry of Defence, carrying on dancing as "demonstrator" for a friend who taught for Arlene Phillips at the London Pineapple Dance Studio. I enjoyed my time with the MOD and finished up as project manager designing a networked computer system for Defence Sales. After leaving the MOD I studied transpersonal psychology with Ian Gordon-Brown and Barbara Somers, and had a practice working with dreams until I moved out of London in 1999.

I've been fortunate in this life to work with many friends such as Caitlin & John Matthews, Emma Restall Orr, Lilla Bek, C Maxwell Cade, Rose Gladden, Colin Bloy, Paul Devereux, Michael Poynder, Tom Graves, Hamish Miller, Vicky Wall and Theo Gimbel. I was part of Fountain International and the Ley Hunter as well as working on The Dragon Project with Dr Don Robins during 1977/8. I studied Alice Bailey's work for many years with the Lucis Trust.

I live now on the borderlands between Wales and England by the river Wye. The name Merlin takes here is Dyfrig. It feels very good to be living in his land and that of one of the mother-rivers of Britain. I share my home with my husband, two cats and a host of wildlife; I paint, read, spin, knit and weave; we garden and grow our own veg … and I write.

Elen Sentier
www.elensentier.co.uk

Moon Books invites you to begin or deepen your encounter with Paganism, in all its rich, creative, flourishing forms.